Unwatered Seeds

Unwatered Seeds

Poems

William Waters

Cherry Grove Collections

© 2024 by William Waters

Published by Cherry Grove Collections
P.O. Box 541106
Cincinnati, OH 45254-1106

Some of these poems appeared previously as follows:
The Saint Ann's Review: "Parting" and "Something Green Growing"
The Blue Mountain Review: "A Thing"
Founder's Favorites: "As Simply as I Know It"
Brief Wilderness: "After" and "Answering Machine Poem" as "Downhill Score"
CALLIOPE: "3:00 A.M."
Here Comes Everyone: The Tomorrow Issue: "But Did"
Halcyon Days: "No Wind Now"
The Ocotillo Review: "Tumbling"
Pennsylvania Literary Journal: "Noch Immer Gegenwärtig"
50 Haikus: "So Much Moves"

COVER ART: "Fonts and Fruits" by William Waters

ISBN: 9781625494627

Poetry Editor: Kevin Walzer
Business Editor: Lori Jareo

Visit us on the web at www.cherry-grove.com

For you

CONTENTS

Acknowledgements	ix
Parting	11
A Thing, Not an Idea	12
As Simply as I Know It	13
After	14
Answering Machine Poem	15
3:00 A.M.	17
But Did	18
Contradictions	19
No Wind Now	20
Tumbling	21
Believable Assertions	22
Noch Immer Gegenwärtig	23
Trying to Burn Away the Rain	30
Before They Light Our Way	31
So Much Moves	32
I Want to Call It Sex	33
Something Green Growing	35

Acknowledgements

I'd like to thank Kathleen Longwaters and Robert Long for their continual support. Kathleen, my poetry partner ever since we started trading poems back in Orono, selflessly uses her careful reading, subtle mind, and gentle spirit to workshop the best out of my texts. Bob, my scotch drinking buddy, continues to support me with years of love, wisdom, enthusiasm, and advocacy.

I'd also like to thank Amy Lipke for reading and commenting on an earlier version of this manuscript. Over the years, Amy has read many of my poems and has provided her likes and dislikes in a way that has helped me clarify and improve them.

I also owe gratitude to many friends who have read and commented on versions of these poems along the way. In particular— Vanessa, Marcos, Bobbie, Mark, and Juliana Snapper enthusiastically responded to drafts and encouraged my continued pursuit of this chapbook. Juliana Snapper, an underwater opera singer, has additionally provided me endless inspiration.

Parting

Today's slow rain
dropping on oak
leaves:
          ...two
wet lips,
      parting.

A Thing, Not an Idea

Her smell
on my skin,
a thing
not
an idea—
nothing
as con-
torted
as love,
but an
acci-
dent of
atoms
contin-
uing.

As Simply as I Know It

To put it physically,
there is a piano wire coming from my stomach,
just below my belly-button;
You strike it with a hammer
and I shake.

After

When the rains came
We both felt better

"I'm sorry," I said, "I didn't…"
"I know," she said, "I…"

And we stopped

Holding hands.

Answering Machine Poem

There is no record of us
    nothing to say
        we were
            young and hot in flesh;

There was that rain then
    and this thirst now—

    but nowhere is there

        a carved stone
        that promises to believe.

I try to remember
    what you felt like laughing
    against my skin

I try to remember
    how those muscles trembled
    and trembled more for trembling some

I try to remember
    exactly how your back arched and turned
    when I kissed you there

but there is only
> these dry leaves moldering
> under another slow rain.

3:00 A.M.
For Daniela

He's asleep already;
finished, rolled over,
and slipped away.

My eyes are closed,
but I'm wide awake
listening to
his breathing;

Even with
my eyes closed
I feel the room
dark; nothing
moves as I
exhale, drift on.

I wish
I were
something light
that flies
wherever it wants,
that lands
without bending
a branch.

But Did

You did not want to
but did

not say
until you had.

Contradictions

Let us each
remain
a
way;

you
the wheel
that grinds the steel
sharp;

I
the steel
that cuts the wheel
round;

let us each
remain
a
part.

No Wind Now

No wind now;
Just drips

from a leaf
hitting
a puddle.

Memories move
memories.

Sleep returns.

Tumbling

Tumbling
Tumbling
Tumbling…

There are no sides to reach out to;
There is no bottom to hit

The place we left
is gone;
The place we are headed to
doesn't exist

Everything in between
is thin
and can't manifest

She points at my heart
with a finger
that's missing, asks:
"Does it hurt?"

I try to tell her
it is all a dream—
But
I have
no mouth

Believable Assertions

When you are too tired to argue
it doesn't matter
if you're alone.

Noch Immer Iegenwärtig[1]
For Gabi

Too many
glasses
of wine,
and now,
I can't
sleep;

It doesn't
help
that he
snores.

I wonder
if I should
get up—
have
a smoke,
read
a book,
take
a walk.

I'm too
tired
to walk,

---

[1] The German translates to "still always present." This is adapted from a Zen saying: 如在 *Nyo Zai: as if one is still there*; even after a person has passed away, for better or worse, we often feel as if that person haunts us.

to anxious
to read
or smoke,
so I
roll over,
think
about
the beginning
again.

Dinner
was perfect.
I think
that is
what made me
feel
so brave—
made me
ask: "Why
don't you
love me?
What's wrong
with us
being
a couple?"

I don't
remember
what he
said—
just that
it sounded
selfish:
boytalk for
"Leave me
alone."

That's when
I had
my second
glass
of wine.

He
was talking
about his
friend's band—
about how
we should
see them
Thursday night;

I started
to remind him

Tuesdays and Thursdays
I go
to the dojo,
have been
for two years
now,
but then
I realize
he thinks
my karate
is something
I do
to entertain
myself
when he's
not here.

I had
a third—
or was it
a fourth—
glass
of wine.

He said
we should
go;

He had
things
to do
in the morning.

Driving home
I stared
out the window:

There was
a couple
running toward
a movie theatre.

She stopped
said something—
I could see
her lips
moving;
He stopped
turned around
and came back;

He held
out his hand
she took it;
they started
running again—

laughing.
I started to cry
but stopped.

Lying here
I try
to imagine
us running—
hand-in-hand,
I try
to imagine
how
it would
feel...

That's when
I feel
the tug
on my arm,
hear him
say: "Hurry up
we've got
to go."

That's when
I know

tomorrow
I will
pack
a small bag,
get the paper,
look for
an apartment.

Trying to Burn Away the Rain

He talks mad
talking love,
trying to burn away the rain
match by match.

Before They Light Our Way...
For Nina Eidsheim

New moons are hard to see
Inch-thin slivers of light,
Noticeable only
As something different.

So Much Moves

I am watching you talk:
so much moves
before your mouth
opens

I Want to Call It Sex

I want to call it sex
    though
        that's not exactly true;

my lying on top of you
    you
        rolling over me,

—our panting and parting
    is more
        of a struggle than that;

        though not so much
            between ourselves

        (there is too much
           fondness
              there)
but rather
    from within—
        where
            we try to act

            like naked angels
            lying in the snow

                    titillated
                    by the cold,
                    but afraid

it will go
        too deep
                last
                    too long;

So, even as my belly rubs your back

                and even as your sweat puddles mine

                —we pant and part,
                but keep our mittens on.

Something Green Growing
For Snapper

I look for you in my dreams
Things are murky
There are waves and water and whales in the way;
Just off stage
I hear you
Singing:
It sounds like a blade of grass
Cracking
The asphalt open

☙ Colophon ❧

This book was printed by Cherry Grove Collections, 2024.

The body text was set in 12 pt. Adobe Garamond Pro, with titles set in 20 pt. Adobe Garamond Pro.

An Adobe Originals design, Adobe Garamond Pro is a digital interpretation of two different fonts: the Roman types of the sixteenth-century French printer, publisher, and type designer Claude Garamond and the italic types of Robert Granjon.

Garamond employs expansive ascenders and descenders, a sharp turn at the top left of the lower case 'a,' and Roman square capitals. This extremely graceful, refined old style typeface, known for its "invisibility," has become a timeless staple for desktop publishers worldwide for its high degree of readability.

Made in the USA
Coppell, TX
23 August 2025